Advance Praise for *What to Carry Into the Future*

What to do in the aftermath of one crisis, while witnessing another in slow motion, and while bracing for yet another? In her "quiet choices of living," Landers gifts readers with incandescent poems that illuminate New York City. At first glance, the book reads like a masterful collection of concrete observations and matter-of-fact genealogies of power. But it quickly reveals itself to serve, too, as an incisive, reflexive series of meditations on ways of knowing, and thus, living with meaning against the seduction of nihilistic despair. Each of the book's three sections is a masterful rendering of the landscapes it habits—with short, propulsive lines swaying the reader down subway train tracks, clusters of lines like blades of grass popping up through cracks in the sidewalks, and a combination of flowing prose and capacious sonnets with the authority of water. The poems do more than flout facile binaries of the urban and the pastoral, blight and life; they provide a polyphonic ode to place as more-than-human life. Landers simultaneously dwells in this political moment and transcends it, inviting readers to grieve with her for those dying and the earth and ourselves—to engage in the act of witness, of attention, and to take one more step, and then another.—*Celina Su*

Sue Landers' latest book is a stunning meditation on sobriety and aftermath. Here, the poet revels in new forms of attention as she rides the subway through New York's underground landscapes, only to surface, notebook in hand. Here, a train ride becomes not a poetic trope, but a 'frame' through which we glimpse the "old names we have for each other." Daring the reader to follow her as she goes toward beauty, holding it "like a compass," *What We Carry Into the Future* updates the urban-pastoral travelogue with a sober memoir that focuses its lens on this collapsing empire's "cathedral of vaulted grime."

—-*Joey Yearous-Algozin*

From the Bronx to Coney Island, through everyday joys and catastrophes, Sue Landers delivers an expansive vision of New York in its many voices and reveries. A lovely companion for your next commute or meditative stroll. *—Jeremiah Moss*

Landers' virtuosic new book merges personal reflection, micro-history, instruction, field notes, and *dérive* to re-invent the City and Subway Poem for our post (post) COVID moment. In three suites of undulating poetry and prose, *What to Carry Into the Future* guides the reader through aftermaths of New York City entanglements with war, revolution, white supremacy, and corporate American values. Opening with an epic subway ride towards opposite ends of the system's map, Landers' speaker first unblurs key neighborhoods' demarcations between consumption and destruction, and then, above ground, navigates the overlooked histories of environmental racism and resilience among marginalized communities living along the shorelines of NYC's major bodies of water. In this urban poetics of care and listening to Place, Landers generates a warmth and immediacy through an engagingly variable line that pulsates with the currents of a dialogically "ice-scratched, roving, and still" eco-consciousness. Furthering the avant-garde probings of U.S. American poets Lorine Niedecker, William Carlos Williams, Frances Chung, and the late Lyn Hejinian, Landers' poetry also draws upon the sublimities of the great Tang dynasty poets Du Fu, Li He, and Li Shangyin. What to carry into the future? The reader would do well to start with this pioneering, dazzlingly bravura work. *—Paolo Javier*

WHAT TO CARRY INTO THE FUTURE

Also by this author

Franklinstein
Covers
248 mgs., a panic picnic

WHAT TO CARRY INTO THE FUTURE

SUSAN LANDERS

ISBN: 979-8-9915011-0-1
Library of Congress Control Number: 2024949651

Cover photo: Chris Turgeon/unsplash
Author photo: Mónica Félix
Book design: Deborah Thomas

NEW YORK STATE OF OPPORTUNITY. Council on the Arts This book is made possible, in part, by the New York State Council on the Arts with the support of the office of the Governor and the New York State Legislature.

Roof Books
are published by Segue Foundation
300 Bowery Fl 2
New York, NY 10012
seguefoundation.com & roofbooks.com

Distributed by Independent Publishers Group/IPGbook.com

Contents

What we call a city is a succession of wildly different places in the same location.

—Rebecca Solnit
Nonstop Metropolis:
A New York City Atlas

My Quotidian Icon

The subways could be anywhere because a state of unhearingness prevails there; unless there is an emergency, and people begin to speak.

—Simone White

But I want nothing this society's got.
I'm going underground.

—The Jam

New York City, 2017–2018

It's common in dystopias for people to go underground to survive after all possibilities on the surface have been exhausted. To go underground is to separate oneself from the most basic indicators of direction and time. Without stars or the sun, any natural sense of direction or time is lost.

From their very beginning, the trains offered New Yorkers a new way to live.

At Hoyt,
the route emblem,
a bullet,
appears—
blue. Jay
and a man's
shirt says,
it's not
where you land,
it's how you
get there. High
street, rattle
cough—
the A train
on its tracks,
balanced—
that moment
before toppling.
Wall Street,
where a man
shoots at things
on his phone.
Chambers, strangers
minding their own
business. Canal,
a beginning
to step into
—Spring,
seashells for a ceiling.
The grates
at West 4th St.
exposing the system
that holds us—
light in the gaps,
a gasp.

A little girl kicks
her brother through Penn
to the end of Times
Square, bulbs
in the breach
through Columbus
where we are held
momentarily
before momentum
blurs reflection
and the tracks split
open a kaleidoscope
past 125th Street
where a boy sells Welch's
till 175th and a man
slips me a piece of paper
that says *donate*
with a curlicued d,
like the arches
of 181st Street,
where I'm alone
and holding
momentarily
at Dyckman
because of train
traffic ahead of us
—a staggering,
a long pause
before lumbering
into Inwood
where it is written
in glacial script
on Manhattan schist:
attend to this place,
now, before it's gone.

Ⓐ

In Inwood Hill Park
near where Sarah Fox's
body was found in 2004
strewn with tulip tree petals,
reward signs still ask
for clues that may lead
to the arrest of her murderer.
The *liriodendron*.
Native to the region,
the tree's flowers
are bright yellow
with orange flares.
Fallacy says it was here,
under Manhattan's
largest tulip tree,
that Peter Minuit "bought"
the island from the Lenape.
A real boulder now sits
in the mythic tree's place,
a place named
Shorakapok,
the wading place,
between the ridges.
Some years ago,
someone was chopping
down trees in the park.
Authorities called it
arboricide, the act
of a serial tree killer.
Chopped down and left to rot:
the bitternut hickory,
some pines, the red oak,
a Kwanzan cherry,
some sugar maples,
the hackberries.

Ⓐ

In 2012, authorities
linked DNA from the site
of Sarah Fox's murder
to DNA found on a chain
used by Occupy protesters
to prop open a subway gate.
Free rides in response
to fare hikes and racist policing.
The DNA was later found
to be that of the lab tech
who worked both cases.
To be in possession
of evidence,
a chain of custody.
I'm drawing lines
to help me see
how I live in such a city.
Hunger Game ringtones
echo through Fort Greene
and its war heroes
till Utica, meaning
old town, a story
that's been told before
and full of gaps.
The express train
through East New York,
where speculators
trade in futures,
change in their favor,
a frenzy. But the pace
in Ozone Park
is steamy, hazy.
Concrete elephants
draped in plastic
marigolds.

I'm eating doubles at Trini City
for $1.25 a piece,
when Twitter tells me
a Russian tycoon
offered a president's son
dirt on a woman who would
never be president,
and he said,
if it's what you say it is,
I love it, especially in summer.
The flags
hang slack
in cul-de-sacs,
as shocking as
a hurricane.
Back on the train,
a little girl is learning to read
a book about Frank and Stella—
they may be pigs.
The little girl is learning
what the word potential means,
what exists in possibility,
what is only unreal
for the time being.
Near me, a man's shirt
reads *100% American*.
No potential in him.
The pigs are already bacon.
Through greasy windows,
I see Euclid's smudgy lilac tiles
—Euclid of what splits
and leaves no remainder—
till we break open
into the light of Big Egg
and Little Egg Marsh.

Ⓐ

Porous boundaries.
Big muck a gateway
for egrets and wires.
I'm eating fish tacos,
$3.25 a piece, on the beach
just days after a fire
burned at 148th Street
for two hours, injuring nine.
Hoyt speculated.
Schermerhorn made rope.
Their station served
as a backdrop in *The Wiz*.
After Michael Jackson died,
there was a proposal
to rename Hoyt-Schermerhorn
after him, but the MTA refused,
saying it would confuse riders.
Two days before he died,
the MTA sold the naming rights
for the Atlantic Pacific station
to Barclays Bank, a corporation
that had once been a family
of enslavers. Barclays,
the arena above the station,
was built on razed
private property seized
through eminent domain.
The opening game at the arena
was postponed because of a hurricane,
Sandy. Technically, Sandy
was a post-tropical cyclone,
a superstorm.
Such classifications
mean different things
to the insurers than the insured.

Ⓐ

When water is whipped
higher than high tide
it's called a surge.
Coastal areas
like the Rockaways
were hit hard by Sandy
when storm surge
knocked out power
causing fires that leveled
whole blocks to ash.
In lower Manhattan
where the surge
took out power,
only the Goldman Sachs
tower remained lit,
thanks to a private
generator subsidized
by public funds after 9/11.
Two months after 9/11,
a plane went down
in the Rockaways.
It was morning,
just after rush hour.
The hole downtown
was still burning.
I thought it was
happening all over again.
The crash killed everyone onboard
and five on the ground.
Most of the passengers came
from Washington Heights,
the other end of the A line,
and the plane crashed in Belle Harbor,
where some of the first responders
on 9/11 had lived.

At Rockaway Park,
a memorial commemorates
the tragedy. A stone
for each life lost.
A doorway into an ocean.
This city's mud bloody grief.
It took years
to reopen South Ferry
after Sandy, a closing
that happened just weeks
after the station
finished years
of 9/11-related repairs.
A mechanic
on the 1 train
tells me,
there's always
more work
to do
to stop the flood.
In the air,
the faint smell of smoke.
Then there's some
rattle garble
about a signal or a switch
on the intercom.
It's midmorning,
summer,
and I'm riding the train
for the wanting
of writing.
I live in a country
that makes poor people
shit between cars,
in the dark.

A 1

Last night
around midnight,
the witching hour,
when tomorrow
becomes today
and today yesterday,
a few representing the many
tried to take our health care away.
Again.
Yesterday,
or was it today,
they were betting
that enough of us
are poor enough
that they can feed on us.
Inside the East River
the tunnel keeps
the water at bay
till Wall Street,
where a triple witching hour
refers to an increase
in volatility
after certain
securities expire
on set dates and times.
This is chaos,
by design.
The subway
is a frame
for refining
one's vision,
a means of focusing
one's seeing
on a time and a place
where people in power

❷

are not just not making sense
but striking sense with all
of their might while I am
wanting to make sense
of my life through the portals
of light formed by the elevated
tracks. Look—
see how it pours—
the light—
into New Lots
full of sunflowers
absorbing the heavy
metals from this earth—
hyperaccumulators
—holding on.
There's a place for us.
That's the melody
the trains play
as they rev up.
How many things are
like and unlike another.
Metaphor, that near miss
of two things and in the gap
—a longing to connect.
Some people can't ride the train
because there are no elevators,
or they can't get a swipe.
People in power often talk
about keeping things
simple:
the one-pager,
the bullet point,
the bottom line.
They love
an express train.

❸

The governor just put out a call
to nonexperts for ideas
on how to fix the trains.
He's offering a million dollars
to the person who can find it—
the big idea that will save the system.
I've always loved New York
because there's always
someone somewhere
close enough
to hear you scream.
In an early draft
of his song "Somewhere,"
instead of living,
Sondheim wrote,
"We'll find a new kind of *city*."
I'm on a bridge
looking at bridges.
Of the melody,
he said it was difficult
to let himself let
the article "a"
just linger there.
A, an indefinite article.
A segue to meaning.
To linger there
longer than is necessary
—unless, of course, it is.
On the jetty,
I meet a woman
in a not-all-who-wander-are-lost
t-shirt who tells me riding the trains
to write poems serves no purpose—
you can circle around and around
but at some point, you must land.

3 B

She asks me
to take off my glasses,
to put down my phone,
and hold out my arms.
She says she's going to press
down on my arms.
I tell her
I won't do any
of those things.
The train
as frame
as alphabet,
routine,
like breath
you forget
until in variation,
you receive
the gift of it
—language,
a city,
the Bronx
in the rain,
is a song
sung from cliffs.
Slick brick,
fedora,
próximo-next.
The Bronx in the rain
is a definite article,
the continent's eruption,
the one that climbs
all day long big sky
and boulder,
perpetually praising
its angels.

B

See what gives
just enough,
C, the local,
the long haul,
the slow pace
of practice
sees in repeating
what went before it
unseen.
The local
is a habit
I don't want
to break.
The local,
a deep lean.
It takes a minute
and gives one back.
Into its reservoir,
settle in
to its low moan.
The C train,
a lulling,
an ease
like mud
folding in
on itself.
This may be
a love letter.
These may be my vows.
About that prenup
we never ironed out,
it doesn't matter.
You always win,
New York.
You always get
whatever you want.

C D

But I can still lay
tracks inside you,
reinscribe in lines
the old names
we have for each other—
Atlantic, Pacific—
how the maiden names stick,
familiar as an ocean,
along the elevated track.
Panadería taekwondo
the Verrazano
dungarees and smokestacks
nail salon and scaffold
right down to your edges
where the dragonflies
and sunflowers wave
monstrous to tomatoes
outside the chop shop
an empty Listerine bottle
and the smell of fresh-baked
bread over Coney Island
Creek where the men
gutting porgies
for chum turn to me
and say, *they are big*
and beautiful
just like you
under a summer sky
quilted by cranes
a woman tears
open an air conditioner.
And it's a beautiful day
for a game
of running
around and around
to get home.

D

The doors open
and a man says he *doesn't want*
to sleep on the train anymore.
The doors open
and a stranger asks me if I have children,
and I stop myself from telling her
I was so busy working
I hardly noticed when blood
stopped releasing from my body,
how far away I was from the workings
of my body while I was working
in a city full of bodies
moving like a hurricane.
The doors open
and the streets
are flooded in Texas.
The doors open
and people are waving from rooftops.
The doors open
and a president pardons
a sheriff who videotaped
women in bathrooms,
the women arrested
for not being born here.
The doors open
for a man in an I'm-not-arguing-
I'm-just-explaining-I'm-right t-shirt,
and a woman asks me
for help with her naturalization test.
She asks me to read aloud the words,
Are you willing to take up
arms in defense of this country?
The doors open
and a man in a Vegas
hotel room kills 60 people
with 15 semiautomatic rifles.

Last night,
there was a hurricane,
then another one.
Some of this isn't metaphorical.
Look up
before it gets darker,
the clouds are gorgeous
and damning.
To get far away
by not stopping
underground in the dark.
I like it, to be like that,
to be so far gone.
But then a horn blares
on the track, a long wail.
Warnings
down the car
then a staggering.
Warnings for the workers
in the tunnels working
to keep the water
at bay from us,
we, who curse
the slowing down,
the stumbling
that trips up the pace
of our rushing that keeps
us at bay from this earth
and our bodies.
Ten days before
the hurricane, the president
lifted restrictions
protecting cities
from floods.
This isn't prophecy,
it's design.

Climate change deniers
want enough of us
at risk enough
that they will never grow
rich enough
selling us
their toxic solutions.
A flashing of lights,
a clattering of tongues.
This local just turned express.
What are the words
to that song again?
I crashed your car
into the bridge.
I don't care!
I love it!
Rain slick city,
city of vanish and stick,
I just want to ride your rocking
with all the other empaths
and nanas, witches
and cynics, the pharmacists,
the squatters,
the haulers of stuff,
as if there were no time left
but all of it,
a continuous present
attending to the unanswerable
question of this city.
Later, in Coney Island,
I meet the great-granddaughter
of the man who made The Whip
and The Tickler—Lisa,
with shooting stars
on her arms.

F

She tells me how T—p's father
bought Steeplechase Park in the 60s
and threw a big party where bikini-clad
women handed out bricks. Bricks
to bust out the glass of the park's
magnificence. He told his guests
to break Steeplechase Park into bits.
The hurricanes approaching
the Caribbean this week have surpassed
all established parameters.
Winds so strong
they are technically
beyond Category 5
and yet there is no Category 6.
There is no Category 6
and, yet, the 185 mile-per-hour
winds of Irma exist.
Chaos might mean
without a library.
Dumbstruck, a leveling.
Chaos, an unpredictable
behavior, appearing random,
can actually be owed to small changes
in conditions over time.
I'm riding a train,
the G train, whose window
is held in place with duct tape.
I remember after 9/11,
or, maybe, it was the blackout,
or Hurricane Irene or Sandy,
I forget, but I remember
they told us to buy duct tape.
I don't know what we were supposed
to use it for—everything,
I suppose—and we are.

F G

I'm feeling this persistent
transition and bend into its
crescent, the silt and the shift.
I fantasize about lying to a man
who makes fizzy water in Canarsie.
I'm taking the L to Canarsie
to visit a seltzer factory
run by the grandson of the first
seltzer man of New York.
When I called him,
I told him I was writing a book.
He didn't ask what kind,
he just said come over.
On the L, I imagine,
that if he asks,
I'll tell him I'm writing a novel
about a man who breaks up
with his girlfriend and returns home
to work for the family
business in Canarsie.
That's seems so much easier
than explaining how
I quit my job
to write poems
about a subway
everyone hates because
they have to take it
to work every day.
His green bottles
from Czechoslovakia
so thick they lasted 100 years
shelter dozens of intricate
pieces in their nozzles,
little clocks to preserve
the precise moment
when a bubble forms.

J L

I ask him how
he came to take over
his grandfather's business.
He told me he broke up with his fiancé
after college and decided to give
the family business a go.
The L train travels in a straight
line from Manhattan to Brooklyn.
It's so much simpler
to be a novelist
than a poet.
After 9/11,
I took the M train
to work even though
it didn't take me anywhere
near my office.
I caught it hours
before rush hour,
before sunrise,
because it seemed
the least likely train
to get bombed.
The M doubles back on itself
then splits into a spur.
Wild trees in the tracks,
graffiti through leaves,
a storefront church
organ spills onto the fast
shadows of late afternoon
and the bodega's
fruit pyramids.
Let's count clouds
and water towers.
This tunnel's
a gateway
to the moon.

Rocking at Atlantic Pacific,
back again
at the impossible
meeting of oceans.
An alert on my phone
announces an attack downtown:
eight people plowed down
on a bike path by a man
in a truck on Halloween,
and someone says,
There was never a better time
for a parade.
We are getting so good
at living in grief.
Two women sit down
where a man had just been sleeping
beneath an ad for knowing your rights—
one arm of the state advising
how not to get struck down
by a different arm of the state.
I'm on my way
to a rally for elevators,
most stations without them,
even in evacuation zones,
where people are expected to go
in the event of a hurricane.
As the protesters gathered,
a man yells from a passing car,
job haters!
and I knew
I was free.
Sun cymbals
a strobe light
down the car—
the last gasp of day
at Avenue J.

N Q

A clattering
across tracks,
paparazzi.
Leaf graffiti,
a rustling.
Sky like cotton candy.
An ocean of clouds,
a gathering,
my quilt.
To write and ride this light.
Maybe this time
is completely unreal.
Maybe this time
is the realest.
Like the crowd
at Times Square
breaking out spontaneously
into "Bodak Yellow."
I see no traces of Pacific
on the walls of Atlantic Barclays.
It takes no time at all
for a bank to swallow an ocean.
Prospect Avenue,
my first subway station,
a blur, is now rezoned
for high rises with climate control
so there's no reason
to open your windows
and worry about particulate matter
like we did after the towers fell.
A bald man grimaces
as he rises from his seat
at 36th Street, where four years
from now, a man will open
fire on the train
during rush hour.

Q R

And yet somehow
I still have faith
there will always
be another train
behind this one.
Up the stairs
and over the ridge
I'm eating chicken shawarma
with lemonade for $11
when a cop
over his loudspeaker
says *go back to school*,
and four boys
on the overpass
break into a run.
All of a sudden
it's Christmastime
and two days since a bomb
went off in that grim little hallway
in Times Square,
you know the one,
the one with the messages on the ceiling:
Go to work.
Go to bed.
Etc.
It's too real for some people,
they can't stand it,
they can't stand to look up.
Today, Times Square smells
like wet paint.
A glossing over.
Like me being carried away
by the impossible clouds in Corona
over Louis Armstrong's house,
preserved like a time capsule.

R S

His gravelly voice in my head
as a group of strangers walk
under the elevated track
right as a train goes by
and the snow shakes loose—
an impromptu snow globe.
What a wonderful world.
A woman on the S says,
I need a seat, I have cancer,
you can't tell by looking at me,
but I do, wanna see my port?
A man in an I'm-broke-bitch
t-shirt sits under Major Jackson's
poem that reads:
All we want is a metropolis
of Sundays, an empire of hand-holding.
The woman with cancer tells me to
write about all the nice people
on the subway. OK?
It's 10:40 a.m. on December 5th, 2017
where 7th Avenue and Broadway meet
and ads flash *I need help*—then—
Do you want to go to the M&M store?
A bride in the crosswalk
gets her picture taken beneath
the sign over the McDonald's
that reads *Impeach!*
Spectacle bundle.
Like trash inside an oyster shell.
A little iridescent
map of survival.
Next to a sign that reads
Art 4 Food or Gold,
a man blows his nose
into an American flag.

R S 4

How many more stops?
So many of us doing the math
from here to there.
I'm on my way
to the cemetery
where a security guard tells me,
this place gets smaller
the longer you're here.
I'm eating a fried fish sandwich
for $13 on City Island
across from a potter's field
where in two years
one in ten dead New Yorkers
will be buried after COVID surges.
But before all that happens:
candy striper smokestacks
and a song down the car.
I'm high
on elevated tracks
again. The doors open
and Queens is a library.
I'm blushing
under the sheer
shiny globe of it all,
beyond the Sunnyside
of Hell Gate, past the junction,
the reservoir, and Silvercup Studios.
This poem is a time plaza—
a cathedral of vaulted grime—
for anyone who has
ever found,
borrowed,
stolen,
or made the time
to take the long way round.

W 5 6 7

I take the Q
to the S
to the C
to the J
and still get to Jamaica
with seven minutes to spare
to catch the last Z train
of the day.
And there,
I wait,
until an old gray train
pulls into the station.
My last train.
But on its emblem,
the bullet,
is the letter J.
So I ask the conductor
if there's a Z
behind this one
and he says,
This J is the Z.
It's the same train.
They're all the same.
Get on.

SIDEWALK NATURALIST

Only in regular contact with the tangible ground and sky can we learn how to orient and navigate in the multiple dimensions that now claim us.

—David Abram

Opened up my eyes
Taught me how to see
Notice every tree—
Notice every tree…

—Stephen Sondheim

Brooklyn, 2022

Here, at the Avenue H subway stop, an oddity: bronze rocking chairs, engraved to look like wood and wicker, bolted to the floor of the above-ground station, which takes the shape of a small house with a wrapping porch.

The station agent comes outside for a smoke and turns to where I'm sitting on a bronze chair and says, *you know, the men who sit here on the porch all day and drink—they pee on those seats.*

Across
from the porch
a string of trees
I'll come to know
by name:

thornless honey locust,

dawn redwood,

(the effusive) sweetgum,

golden rain.

mid spring

late summer

early fall

Along the tracks,
trees define time
with features
of seasonal interest:

red bud clusters,

the dogwood's fake flowers,

the peeling planes.

Common in cities, plane trees remove pollutants
from the air. They filter particulates.
Resistant to breaking, they shed their skin,
bark peeling in sheaths.

I'm remembering
what May Sarton said:

Imitate the trees.
Learn to lose
in order to recover.

Its habit
is the form
a tree takes.
The dawn redwood,
a witch hat.
Not evergreen,
but ancient,
this living fossil
from a hundred million years ago.
This wild canvas,
the dawn redwood
was once thought to be extinct,
missing for millennia
until it was spotted,
in rural China
in the 1940s.
Stalwart,
the deciduous conifer
with needles unfurled.

What if we can
—what if we choose to—

go
toward beauty,

to hold it,
like a compass

to have it guide us
through this—

—what is this?

A continuous aftermath.

late winter

early spring

Across time
a slow growth
extends
into forms
unforetold:

the trees

and their slow

motion into abundance

Is the honey locust a good tree?

Lining either side of the block
framed by apartments,
the old women on their walkers
sit beneath its limbs.
Fernlike, but not, the locust
is Fabaceae (the pea)
with flowers inconspicuous
except for one week in summer—
a mild sweetness
then a scattering of catkins.
It does well in bad soil and salt
with plated bark like a book.
I learned its name,
and suddenly
it was everywhere.
Like, but unlike,
the Japanese pagoda,
all green puffs and beaded droplets,
with bark of interlocking ridges,
offering flowers long after
the others have dropped.

A resurgence.

I'm interested in this concept of aftermath,
as in:

the grass
that grows
over mown meadows.

mid summer

early winter

After years
of working
at a screen
at a desk
for hours
every day
as the sirens
rang in the background
and apologizing
every day
to the people
on the screens
for all the things
I couldn't do
because
of all the things
I was busy doing.
After racing
up a mountain
of tasks,

my predilection

for productivity

—radiating out
and reflecting back—

ran out.

And I just—

stopped

quit

hung

in the air

like a cartoon
before falling
down
a metaphorical
cliffside,
only feeling like
I had come
to a full stop
after many days
or maybe weeks
maybe months
of lying on the floor
reading books
about roses
and the attention economy.

late winter

early spring

And only then,
once rested,
did I stand up
and go looking
for somewhere
to be useful.
At the food pantry,
Cecilia pointed me
to one bag
and then another.
She said,
4 beets in a bag.
And so I did that.
Loamy taproots,
an anchor.
Like a tulip tree,
a Mack truck—
solid, straight up,
known knowns
with ridges deep enough
to hold and flowers
in the reaches.

What use is a tulip tree?

Trees sequester carbon dioxide, what fossil fuels spew,
storing carbon in their fibers, a game of keep-away,
even though humans add more CO2 than the trees could
ever hold.

Out of balance,

still—

the trees
persist.

In 2020, emissions decreased when COVID sequestered
many of us inside. In the spring, the streets looked
almost clean. But after a few months, masks appeared
in the gutter,

then plastic bags,

then all the rest

came back

to normal again.

Our normal
is trash.

late spring

early summer

Trellis of clematis,
its suede wallpaper
open to the caterpillars.

Pollen in the sunbeams
by the train tracks
draped in wisteria.

The katsura's little heart
leaves, miniature cymbals,
a delicate shivering.

The sun has a different ease to it now.

A warmth that holds up
the trees planted when
the train tracks were laid.

I'm walking past the exploding
peonies, all messy swagger
beside the hostas, past
the ubiquitous planes, riddled
with their inscrutable maps.

It's Thursday, so along the landscaped
medians of the Flatbush Malls, a queue
of people wait beside the rose bushes
with their grocery carts for the food
pantry on Coney Island Ave. to open.

Outside the bodega, a bald man
shaves his head. Free COVID tests
at the eyebrow threader.
And in the tree pits, honey locusts
stretch out and droop.

On the podcast I'm listening to,
a guest says recovery is the baseline
for caring about your life
and not something
to master.

mid summer

mid fall

early winter

late spring

Buffalo.

Uvalde.

Roe.

How do I write

about rest

in distress?

On the radio, Gessen describes supermodels in a café in Kyiv talking about rape.

What is the habit,

the shape,

of this unthinkable
simultaneity?

Day after day

my perambulation,

my peripatetic practice:

to slow

the fuck

down.

At what point does the pin oak release its tight habit?
Answer: Around 40, it loosens into a canopy.

To fall open

in languid extension

like days lengthening

or surrender.

How much more will be knowable
if I keep returning

to this walk,

this porch,

this thornless honey locust?

Heat-trapping CO_2 is now 50% higher
than at the start of the Industrial Revolution.
The trees alone—

the trees that offer
such glorious reprieve—

will not stop it.

I name that willow
Snuffleupagus.

A sweet gum,
jack rabbit.

My Siberian elms,
the three sisters.

Wild catalpa strews its flowers,
its luscious wells of maroon.
The hop-hornbeam thrives on neglect.
Wind rustles the vase-shaped zelkovas.

A woman in a churchyard
fills her bucket with linden
blossoms known to be good
for congestion.

Two little kids jump
from the base of a giant plane tree
onto the sidewalk. Squealing,
they find the world so new.

Delivery drivers drag their sacks
across the ground, past the plastic
water bottles in the gutter
filled with urine.

After six months of rest, a long-standing
injury no longer flares when I walk.
And I think to myself, what feeling
is *this*? That *absence* of pain?

late spring

late summer

The dogwoods stretch their necks.

The Kentucky coffee bean drops its sticky pods.

A tree of heaven rains down just as I pass underneath.

Is this

Arcadia?

I'm besotted

by this field

by this field note practice.

Holly says sobriety
is paying attention.

Orange tabby in the foxglove.

Four beets in a bag.

The poppy's blocky skeleton.

A net full of mulberries,

sweetest

at the point
they let go.

Untie
the soft knots
of the crochet.

Begin again.

To do one thing
and then another.

Look,
there's a lily.

Look,
there's another one.

Line by line

to build such

tender thoughts.

To know that I'm home.

Like,

really,

even in the gravity of it all.

Siren.

Birdsong.

The train.

Again.

Again.

Butterfly bush.

Blue Bird Rose of Sharon

Buckeye starting to fruit.

Post bloom,

            the golden rain

                        holds up its little lanterns

                        telling me it has changed.

Scattered on the sidewalk—
early green acorns.
This is false autumn.

Under drought conditions,
in heat stress,
the trees release.

A protective measure
the trees take on
to refocus on living.

Every day

we choose

what to carry

into the future.

Today,

there are seed pods

on the honey locust.

And look,

that one

there—

—it has thorns.

WATER FINDS A WAY

Any fool can get into an ocean
But it takes a Goddess
To get out of one.
—Jack Spicer

I sit by and watch the river flow
I sit by and watch the traffic go
—Blondie

New York City, 2023–2024

Atlantic Ocean

In her poem about the Mississippi, Lucille Clifton considers how, in water, *the past is always flowing*. Once a barrier island in the ocean, by the early 20th century, Coney Island had been transformed into a peninsula attached to Brooklyn by landfill. The beach isn't quite original either, with its sand deposited and replenished over time, held in place by structures perpendicular to the shore that protect against erosion. A 2023 study found it's one of the fastest sinking areas of the city. A history full of speculative real estate. Predatory thrills. The ocean's a backdrop for the iconic Wonder Wheel, unusual for its swinging track where carriages roll free as the wheel rotates. This rare type of Ferris wheel—one of only three in existence—is called eccentric.

In the light—in the lush—in the lushness
of light—in summer—in the some times
when there is time—in the nothing
—no thing but in water—
at the edges—at the shelf—I come to read it:
the ocean—a music—impossible
as the wheel turns—an uplifting—glinting
in its blue spin—going round and around
by the shore—a wonder—its gears pressing
into old grooves like a known thing but still
a new thing—this clicking—that swinging—
that makes me feel like I could always have
—that makes me feel like I could
never lose—this feeling of freedom.

Gowanus Canal

Development around the Gowanus has been swift since a rezoning in 2021, so seismic that some locals have wondered if the neighborhood's eccentricities will survive. Going up around the canal—on land classified as brownfields—are dozens of high rises with limited affordable housing. For decades, gas plants, tanneries, and oil refineries dumped toxic waste into the Gowanus. Declared a Superfund site in 2010, the actual cleanup began ten years later and will take many more to complete. Today, an ongoing source of pollution in the canal is combined sewer overflow—that combination of raw sewage and stormwater that strains the sewers so much that the system's failsafe is to redirect it into waterways. A manmade wetland on one corner of the canal—branded sponge park—filters stormwater runoff to some degree. This reminds me of Lorine Niedecker calling her watery world *soft and serious*. Lorine, reinscribing the places she loved.

A creek off the bay.
A salt marsh.
There had been oysters.
The water brackish.
Named after some say a Canarsie leader.
Then grids atop coal ash and trash.
The carving of channels for industry heavy.
A century of discharge.
Today's black mayonnaise.
Bankside a condo with Superfund terrace.
Excavators in the canal now, a dredging.
Beside the wildflowers in the ballasts:
hibiscus on the lift bridge,
the bushes teeming with rosehips.

Newtown Creek

A boulder marks the start of the path along Newtown Creek, a trail cairn. Cairn, a tether to stillness before or after effort. The boulder born of fire cooled had been transported by an ice sheet over ten thousand years ago. Workers laying a waterline in the neighborhood found it nearby. I began writing this book in 2017 after quitting a job, then paused writing it after starting another. While not writing, I told the poet Ryka Aoki that I had run out of things to say. She told me *writing isn't a reservoir, it's a river*. For decades, oil seeped into Newtown Creek from nearby refineries. Its cleanup remains unfinished. In 2021, around the time the first COVID vaccine rolled out, when it seemed possible to imagine a future again, the Newtown Creek Nature Walk opened. Part art, part park, part green infrastructure, the path winds around the largest sewage treatment plant in the city, a collage of the organic and industrial. Ryka reminded me I had a choice to return to the flow.

Poetry gave me a reason to walk
across a bridge emulating a boat
over the wastewater resource recovery
facility, its effluence masked by sumac.
To write is a reason to go to the tributary,
to the affluent keeper of bladderwrack
and muck. To appreciate all that is wild
and all that is not by the Superfund site,
the sludge digester, the Pleistocene rock.
Creek like a comma between boroughs.
Crickets in the horsehair, the scouring rush.
It turns out I want to write like a glacial
erratic—the rock that wanders—
ice-scratched, roving, and still.

Coney Island Creek

In an essay about New York City's water supply systems, Celina Su wrote *to take after water is to adapt to context, but also to thirst for depth, for belonging... When we are all relations, the future is estuary*. Estuary a passage. From the Latin to boil, a rapid phase of transition. Coney Island Creek, the last remnant of a salt marsh estuary, connects residential and industrial areas; marshland and parks; people, birds, and bay. A collage. Polluting industries left a toxic legacy, and as recently as 2016, a local apartment complex was dumping raw sewage into the creek. Attempts to get it declared a Superfund site have so far been unsuccessful, but the community continues to fight. The Superfund program today has less funding than it did in 1981. Even so, the park where the creek meets the bay is an active gathering spot. Where blue meets blue, an ease.

Estuary with fish tang, a funk. Pluff mud.
Decayed spartina grass and sewage.
I smell the creek before I see it,
greeted by an egret flying low to its perch.
Nearby ship ribs rise, a ghostly flotilla
—underwater wrecks tucked
inside this soft barrier of salt marsh.
People in the water, too—
fishermen, swimmers, a baptism.
Volatile organic compounds can't
keep them away. The seekers,
they play, while the black locust trees
chatter beside this once tidal strait—
precarious, resilient, unfurling.

Spuyten Duyvil Creek

Technically a short tidal estuary, Spuyten Duyvil Creek connects the Harlem and Hudson rivers. It runs between the Bronx and Manhattan, the products of continental shifts millions of years ago that exposed bedrock. Bedrock, that which holds up what is loose. The eruptions of gneiss, marble, and schist along the creek's path differentiate the area's landscape. The outcrops form a visual vocabulary of all times combined. Vocabulary, that which is remembered. Prepositions, a part of speech, reveal relations, cohere like water.

Where the devil spews a current
and the crow caws under the high-rise
past the swing bridge where the train
horns blow and the osprey hunts
on the rocky promontory inside the glacial
potholes where marble lies beneath the schist
above a witch hazel understory between
the ridges in the wading place beside
the cove and the night heron's mudflat
near the scullers the recovered marsh
the place of the reeds the flooded path
the glistening place where I saw that rat
and the sandpiper released its metallic spink
at the tip of the island on my day off.

Gerritsen Creek

Brooklyn's largest park is not Prospect, but Marine, part tidal marsh, where the living thrive in the liminal. Gerritsen Creek starts as a freshwater stream (now storm drain) and flows through the marsh past a small beach into Jamaica Bay. Most of the bay's original marshes have been filled in by development or lost to erosion caused by rising sea levels and nitrogen from local sewage plants. Marine Park's salt marsh went through a major restoration in 2012, which re-established its mosaic of grasses and shrubs. An alliance of volunteers continues the cleanup. It's an ongoing process, this recovery.

After the Doobie Brothers, after the jet ski,
after the trucks rumble by on the Belt,
after the women grill chicken in a fire pit,
and a teenager casts their line,
after a thin crowd on a slip of sand dwindles
to one man wading thigh-high with a net,
the phragmites in bloom susurrate.
The fiddler crabs play in decay.
Clapper rails chortle their chirp,
and an osprey call cuts like a whistle
through the sumac, the bayberry, the cordgrass,
the car carcass, here, in this place for the hardy,
for the ones that can deal with whatever
the tide brings them and whatever it carries away.

Harlem River

Fifteen bridges cross the Harlem River, an eight-mile tidal straight. Ample paths for fluctuation. Two of them connect Manhattan to Randall's Island. Starting in the spring of 2022, as the city experienced an increase in people seeking asylum, its patchwork system of sheltering newcomers included tents on Randall's Island. A place with a long history of providing—or purporting to provide—refuge to the vulnerable. Sanctuary, what everyone deserves. That stillness before or after effort. A state of balance so that the body can function properly. Balance, an active state, that moment right before toppling—then not.

The river snug, tucked
between island and island, slips
between the highway and a marsh
between hell gates with a history of asylum.
Concrete and scrub shrub.
Perennials add sinuous flow as security
guards come and go at shift change
from the temporary shelters
for ongoing emergencies.
Fishermen catch striped bass
by the combined sewer overflow.
Bridge to bridge to bridge
over and through the littoral zone,
a refuge for those in fluctuation.

Sunset Cove

Broad Channel is the only inhabited island in Jamaica Bay, a slip of land about four blocks wide, also called Big Egg Marsh. Every home there was flooded during Sandy. In 2023, the city opened a park by the water, transforming a polluted marina into a restored saltwater marsh. Sunset Cove, a circular inlet of the Bay. It's part of the Atlantic Flyway, a migratory route for birds. The park's curved pathway was built from a boardwalk recovered from Rockaway Beach after Sandy. Going round and around. A known thing but still a new thing, a murmuration.

A flock of something warbles low
in the distance off Big Egg and Little Egg Marsh.
Between gray day and bay, a cove.
Gulls maybe. Foraging to loaf.
A good life in mudflats.
If I knew the names of birds,
I would say I saw a snow goose.
Brant, coot, or grebe.
Buffleheads, maybe. Yellowlegs, a loon.
An eagle, a starling. Kestrel or wren.
They all come here, you know,
even the glossy ibis, which nests
on the hassock, a tuffet of bog,
known also as Subway Island.

Erie Basin

The Erie Basin in Red Hook had been one of the busiest ports in New York until the advent of container ships after World War II, which were too wide, too deep, and too fast for the port to handle. Maritime artifacts arranged in a park beside the basin offer an abbreviated history. Cranes, ropes, and winches. The park is owned by Ikea, part of its deal with the city to open the company's first local store with the help of tax breaks. To break is to divide into parts, to undo continuity, that which links together a scene without discrepancies.

The swell is the premonition
of a wave, the memory of the fetch,
the fetch where the wind lifts the sea.
Channel to basin, channel to flats.
From channel to bay to harbor.
Stormwater ponds a pothole
patched above a spring.
A buoy bell gongs. A sign
relays what used to happen here:
chock a block to raise a boat,
crane a boom to swing.
To tie a knot a skill and now—
the channel full of cruise ships,
asphalt for a sea.

Bronx River

At Concrete Plant Park beside the Bronx River, volunteers maintain an edible and medicinal foodway, a public space for legal foraging. A place to refuel or to heal. Their work is a continuation of decades of community organizing to restore the river, reclaim access to the waterfront, and reconnect neighborhoods long divided by highways. The park is in the South Bronx, an epicenter of environmental racism, not too far from the river's mouth, where after 23 miles, the river joins with the East River. A confluence. A coming together at Hunts Point, home to the largest food distribution center in the nation and majority supplier of the city's fresh food.

After digging through and digging out
decades of designed division
—the tires, the toxins, debris—
the borough of the Bronx is reconnected,
in places, to its namesake, the river.
To dredge the river, to bridge the land,
to access the mummichog and swamp rose.
In the shadow of the 6 train, a palimpsest:
orange silos emptied of concrete, now sculptures
by the boat launch and chess boards, markers
for a bike path and foodway, a trailway
to forage wild resources—chestnut or goji berry.
Bergamot for mood, chickweed for cough.
Some mugwort to ward off fatigue.

Hudson River

In the 1970s and 80s, the vestiges of the city's industrial history along the Hudson—the ruined piers and warehouses of the west side—became an unregulated, free space for queer cruising, shelter, art, and community. The artist Gordon Matta-Clark's installation there, *Day's End*, in which he cut out large swaths of a warehouse's walls, poured light onto the scene. David Hammons' homage to it, now permanently installed in its place, takes the exposure further. Replicating the same warehouse's outline, its frame, the shell, is just that—empty, distilled.

In a city disinclined to archive itself,
it's not surprising that the Hudson
is as boring as a highway.
River by greenway of asphalt,
a black viscous mixture, the by-product of oil.
All abrupt transition to the impermeable.
Even the ghost pier, the skeletal warehouse,
a gesture toward what once was wild
abandon, seems an empty future.
Where are the great waters in constant motion?
Maybe this is a warning.
Like cypresses, those glorious,
rot-resistant river trees, that can't
grow back if cut too deeply.

East River

War offers another way to frame a city. During the revolution, more than ten thousand Americans died on British prison ships docked in the East River. The stock market opened near the river shortly after the war, part of a plan to help the country cover its debts. The agreement that created the stock exchange is named after the tree where it was signed—the buttonwood, or sycamore, the ubiquitous plane. Two hundred years later, a floating jail opened on the river. For thirty years, the jail barge imprisoned thousands of men—and at one point, children. Another component of the city's racist and inhumane system of incarceration. It closed only in late 2023. *Whatever can happen to anyone can happen to me*, Muriel Rukeyser writes in a poem about the city, a city of change in a nation of war. The river bends near the barge before heading out toward the sound. To sound out, a line of inquiry.

In a drowned valley,
the river's thick ribbons
of gray play in the swell.
A family barbeques beside
the candy cane smokestacks.
Carousels and cormorants.
Gulls, unbothered by boats.
The way a river goes back
and forth is called a meander.
The river, a murky throughline
from the world's largest
stock exchange to its biggest
prison ship, cannot explain
how either continues to exist.

Rockaway Inlet

I was watching the shorebirds feed on Plumb Beach, a small stretch of shoreline between the Belt Parkway and Rockaway Inlet, the strait that connects Jamaica Bay to the Atlantic Ocean, in late 2023, when the poet Mosab Abu Toha shared on his Instagram, *There is a duty that everyone should take on, that they need to write about what they see and feel. It can be about everything. About your dinner with family, your trips to the seashore, watching the sunset, etc. But let Gaza be part of it.*

Beach between a bay and a bay,
a creek, creek, and inlet.
A mudflat lagoon, a dune
with thickets choked by memory foam.
In summer, there will be horseshoe crabs,
but today, plastic roses and razor clams.
Some terns, a plover.
The stretch was once an island
full of people till Moses brought
in bulldozers to build the Belt.
Dead goose in the sand.
Winter's a desolate season.
Inlet to harbor to ocean to sea,
5,673 miles from the genocide in Gaza.

Jamaica Bay

Over the 20th century, Jamaica Bay, a wetland estuary as large as Manhattan, lost most of its marshland. Marshes—reservoirs of carbon, sponges for flood—protect us from harm. Scientists predicted the bay's marshland would be gone completely by 2025 without intervention, which is now underway, but progress is slow. Erode, restore. A park overlooking the bay, named for Shirley Chisholm, the first black woman to run for president, was completed in 2021. The park had been envisioned nearly seventy years earlier. A history of promises and takebacks, dumping and remediation. The paleoecologist Dorothy M. Peteet calls marshes *archives for climate change*. In the muck, a history of human decisions.

As seen from this hill by the bay:
ziggurats of trash now pitch pine and willow.
Sandy-bottom beach recovered from sludge.
The soils of the bay run dark-gray to gray silt,
clay silt to sandy. Silt loam, Malone loam to peat.
Concrete, the birds' clam-slamming ground.
The bay in recovery from marsh loss,
its marshes long drowning in place.
This park was first marshland,
then landfill. Landfill now capped
and off-gassing. Its grasses grow
back after mowing. A process
of returning after injury, an attempt
to recoup what's been lost.

Atlantic Ocean

Again, there's Clifton, considering water *the great circulation*. Eccentricity is a measure of how much an elliptical path deviates from a perfect circle. The eccentricity of a line is infinite. Elliptical can be a leaving out. I don't mean to sound cryptic. What I mean to say is that the city's imperfect and more than it could ever contain. A bedrock, holding up what is loose. A history of human decisions as many as there are ways to love a city. Yes, these are my vows.

To move a handful of sand
from one hand to another.
To repeat. The water
is the same water and still it is new
under the pavilion that smells
like salt and sunscreen and pee,
where an old man passes a strawberry
to another man who nods in thanks.
I am here because the ocean is there.
To look out onto the horizon.
To see, from the edges of the city,
a vista, that which extends beyond
what I know today, and to make
the quiet choices of living.

Acknowledgments

This book came out of a quest to ride every New York City subway from end to end, and transformed into a meditation on joy amidst emergencies. I owe special thanks to my wife who joined me on many of my rides to the end of the line, both real and metaphorical.

Earlier versions of these poems appeared in *About Place Journal*, Academy of American Poets *Poem-a-Day*, *The Brooklyn Rail*, *Three Fold Press*, *Hot Pink*, *The Tiny*, and *Volume*. A limited edition chapbook of "Sidewalk Naturalist" was published by above/ground press.

"My Quotidian Icon" takes its title from a *New York Times* article about the mass shooting on the subway, "Videos Show an Ordinary New York Morning Erupting Into Chaos on the N Train" by Sarah Maslin Nir and Andy Newman, April 12, 2022.

ROOF BOOKS

the best in language since 1976

Recent & Selected Titles

- WINDOWS 85 by Chris Campanioni, 160 pp. $20
- BUMBLEBEES by Deborah Meadows, 100 pp. $20
- THROUGH A WINDOW by Norman Fischer, 104 pp. $20
- SECRET SOUNDS OF PONDS by David Rothenberg, 138 pp. $29.95
- HAND ME THE LIMITS by Ted Rees, 130 pp. $20
- TGIRL.JPG by Sol Cabrini, 138 pp. $29.95
- THE POLITICS OF HOPE (After the War): Selected and New Poems by Dubravka Djuric, Biljana D. Obradovic (translator), 248 pp. $25
- BAINBRIDGE ISLAND NOTEBOOK by Uche Nduka, 148 pp. $20
- MAMMAL by Richard Loranger, 128 pp. $20
- EXCURSIVE by Elizabeth Robinson, 140 pp. $20
- I, BOOMBOX by Robert Glück, 194 pp. $20
- FOR TRAPPED THINGS by Brian Kim Stefans, 138 pp. $20
- TRUE ACCOUNT OF TALKING TO THE 7 IN SUNNYSIDE by Paolo Javier, 192 pp. $20
- THE NIGHT BEFORE THE DAY ON WHICH by Jean Day, 118 pp. $20
- MINE ECLOGUE by Jacob Kahn, 104 pp. $20
- SCISSORWORK by Uche Nduka, 150 pp. $20
- THIEF OF HEARTS by Maxwell Owen Clark, 116 pp. $20
- DOG DAY ECONOMY by Ted Rees, 138 pp. $20
- THE NERVE EPISTLE by Sarah Riggs, 110 pp. $20
- QUANUNDRUM: [i will be your many angled thing] by Edwin Torres, 128 pp. $20
- FETAL POSITION by Holly Melgard, 110 pp. $20
- DEATH & DISASTER SERIES by Lonely Christopher, 192 pp. $20
- THE COMBUSTION CYCLE by Will Alexander, 614 pp. $25
- URBAN POETRY FROM CHINA editors Huang Fan and James Sherry, translation editor Daniel Tay, 412 pp. $25

Roof Books are published by
Segue Foundation / seguefoundation.com
and distributed by Roof Books / roofbooks.com &
Independent Publishers Group / IPGbook.com